Cassiob...

Thirty walks from C...

including

the local nature reserve alongside the park,
Croxley, Whippendell Wood and Chandlers Cross

and

extended walks along the Grand Union Canal
to Rickmansworth and Kings Langley

www.cassiobury-walks.co.uk

CASSIOBURY WALKS

Published by *QUICKTEST* May 2013
www.cassiobury-walks.co.uk

Copyright © Raffi Katz 2013

ISBN: 978-0-9512095-4-7

Mapping (of the park and nature reserve) based on an illustration by Red Mason
Mapping (of the wider area) generated from Open Street Map
The representation of a road, track or footpath is no evidence of a right of way

All rights reserved. No part of this book may be reproduced or transmitted in any form or by other means without permission in writing from the author, except by a reviewer who wishes to quote brief passages in connection with a review written for insertion in a magazine, newspaper or broadcast.

CONTENTS

Key	9
Location and parking	10
The park and surrounding area	15
7 Links	23
Finding the park, finding your way around the park	
5 Walks in the park	29
from 20 minutes to 1 hour	
6 Strolls in the Park	43
Circular walks from an entrance to the park (or the car park) from 6 to 12 minutes	
17 Further Afield	46
Nature reserve, Whippendell Wood, Chandlers Cross, The Grove, Croxley. From 20 minutes to 2½ hours.	
2 Walks along the canal path	82
North past Kings Langley, South past Rickmansworth	
QR codes and URLs	97

GENERAL MAPS OF THE PARK AND SURROUNDING AREA

Watford in relation to Hertfordshire and North London	6
The Park in relation to Watford and Hertfordshire	8
Entrances to the park, and parking	10
The Park	12
The Nature Reserve	14
The picnic benches by the bridges over the river and canal	23

WATFORD IN RELATION TO LONDON AND HERTFORDSHIRE

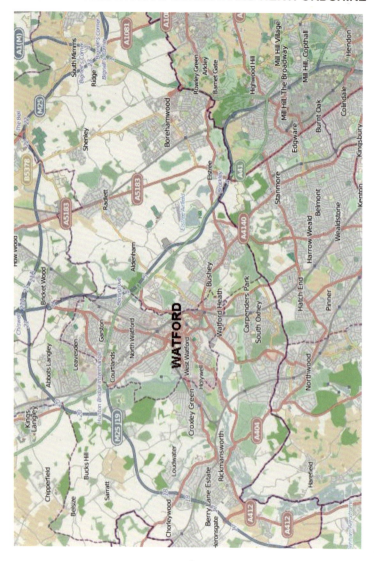

WATFORD? WHERE IS WATFORD?

Watford is in South Hertfordshire, it borders North London to the South and East, with Hemel Hempstead and St Albans to the North, and Rickmansworth to the West.

Cassiobury Park is close to Watford town centre. By car from London, starting at the A41, journey times are: Edgware 17 to 18 minutes; Mill Hill 19 to 20 minutes.

On the slower local roads journey times are: Bushey 10 to 15 minutes; Stanmore, Pinner or Northwood 20 to 25 minutes; Borehamwood or Harrow 25 to 30 minutes; Barnet 35 to 40 minutes.

INTRODUCTION

In 2011 I moved to Watford, near Cassiobury Park.

I like walking, I like writing, I like taking photographs. An idea began to form in my mind. A book of walks, with photographs.

Originally I had intended the walks to take you around the park, through the nature reserve, and along the river and canal – five or six short walks. By 2013 the book had grown to over 30 walks and strolls, lasting from ten minutes to three hours.

I hope you enjoy this little book. If you would like to see more of my photographs, and some extra walks, visit www.cassiobury-walks.co.uk

Raffi Katz, May 2013

ACKNOWLEDGEMENTS

The general maps are open source maps, © *OpenStreetMap contributors*, see www.openstreetmap.org/copyright. The maps of the park and nature reserve are reproduced by kind permission of Watford Council from an original drawing (without text) by illustrator and graphic designer Alan Whitlock, his artwork can be seen on many notices and signs around Watford, see www.redmason.com.

My thanks go to Rob Hopkins of Herts and Middlesex Wildlife Trust for his tours of the nature reserve and Katy Cartmell for designing the cover.

THE PARK IN RELATION TO WATFORD

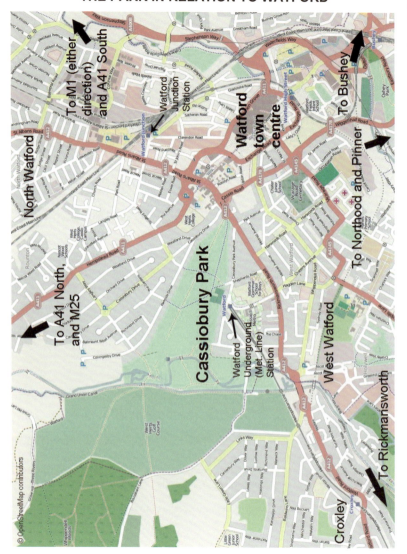

KEY

✹   Starting-point

••••   The route

→   Walk in this direction

✹	**Your location** in relation to roads, railways etc
ff	**Fascinating Fact,** tell your children, amaze your friends.
↩	**Change route / alternative route**
Dtr	**Detour**, usually just a few yards, then walk back to re-join the route
i	**Information**

0	These numbers are minutes *but they are approximate!* That is because not everyone walks at the same speed; it is because *you* might not walk at the same speed (you might slow down as you tire, or speed up if the pub is about to close). There are two reasons for listing minutes: so that you can see how far it is to the next instruction (e.g. 3mns or 25mns) and so that you can see how far you have yet to go.
6	
21	
24	
27	
35	
1:05	

QR CODES (see page 97)

Useful websites (pubs, attractions, local events, extra maps) are marked with a QR code, scan it with your smartphone, or if you are at home in front of a computer, type in the URL (website address). See page 97.

ENTRANCES TO THE PARK, AND PARKING

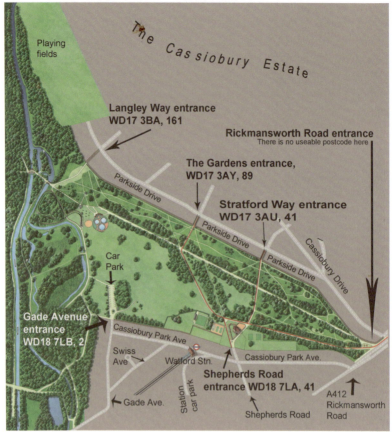

The car park in the park is at the end of Gade Avenue, there is parking for 90 cars in the main car park, plus an overflow for 60 cars if it's not too wet. It is free and is open from 6am to 9pm. There is no exit after 10pm (in emergency call 01923 226400). Please do not confuse this car park with *Gade Car Park*, a multi-storey car park in the town centre.

On the approach to the car park a sign usefully tells you that there is alternative parking in the town, but that's a couple of miles away in the town centre. If the car park in the park is full, you have the following options:

- park in the street near the station, parking restrictions on the single yellow lines are Mon-Fri 9-11am on one side of each road and Mon-Fri 3-4pm on the other side.

- try the station car park: 64 spaces, pay-and-display, Monday to Friday £4.00, Saturdays and bank holidays £2.00, Sundays £1.50. From the car park to the park is a 4 to 5 minute walk (see the map on page 10).

- drive to the Cassiobury Estate on the other side of the park, like this:

From the car park in the park, set your mileometer to zero (0.0) at the exit.

0.0	turn left into Cassiobury Park Avenue
0.6	At the end, the road filters left onto main road (no choice). Stay in left Lane.
0.9	At the roundabout turn left, stay in lane, road bends left, then right, past two big buildings (Leisure Centre and West Herts College) and pedestrian lights.
1.8	Turn left at the second set of lights[1] into Langley Way
1.8	Ahead (2nd exit) at the roundabout then start to look for somewhere to park - from the roundabout the park is a 4mn walk (parking bays on roundabout) - as you pass Trefusis Walk (on your right) the park is a 3mn walk - as you pass Belmount Wood Avenue (on your right) the park is a 2mn walk - as you pass De Vere Walk (on your left) the park is a 1mn walk
2.0	At the end, the Langley Way entrance to the Park is ahead of you, if you still haven't found anywhere to park, turn left (Parkside Drive). The next entrance to the park is opposite The Gardens, and the next is opposite Stratford Way. If you still haven't found a space, continue along Parkside Drive, turn sharp left into Cassiobury Drive, then left at the roundabout and again.

There are restrictions aimed at preventing parking for West Herts College, hence the unusual times: no parking 10.30am to 2.30pm 1 September to 30 June.

Each November there is a Guy Fawkes firework display in the park, it attracts 40,000 visitors, there is no parking near the park and the car park in the park is reserved for Disabled Badgeholders only. Park in any multi-story car park on the ring road, find the Rickmansworth Road, follow the crowds.

---

[1] It's quicker to turn left at the first set of lights into Stratford Road, continue to the very end and turn right into Parkside Drive. But this route is easier for parking.

THE PARK

THE PARK

① Bridge (The Iron Bridge) over the canal (the Grand Union Canal)

② Bridge (The Rustic Bridge) over the river (River Gade) and also the picnic benches where many of my walks start.

Between the two bridges is a weir.

③ Toilets

④ Picnic benches by the playground, plus ice cream van in the summer
Playground (pink circle) – plus a bouncy castle in the summer
Paddling pools (blue circles) – with changing rooms and toilets
Kiosk for tea, ice cream etc - open all the year round
Station for the miniature railway.

⑤ Car park
⑥ Bowls green, tennis and basketball courts
⑦ Café Cha Cha
⑧ The owl tree
⑨ Croquet Lawns
⑩ Tennis courts

A Nature Reserve (there is a detailed map on the next page)

B Steepest hill for sledging, best view for fireworks

C When the funfair comes to town, it's usually here

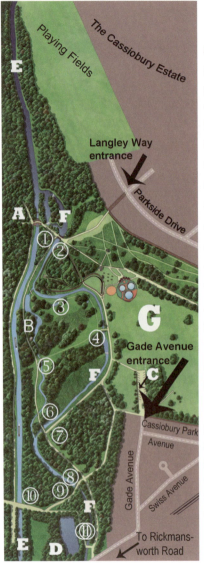

The Nature Reserve

BRIDGES

① The Iron Bridge*

② The Rustic Bridge*

* See detailed map on page 23.

③ Scrape Bridge

④ Meadow Bridge

⑤ Little Meadow Bridge

⑥ Crowfoot bridge

⑦ Pooh Bridge

⑧ Little Kingfisher Bridge

⑨ Kingfisher Bridge

⑩ Rousebarn Lane Canal Bridge

⑪ Ford Bridge

The two bridges at 6 and 7 are almost identical to the two bridges at 8 and 9.

OTHER FEATURES

A Two paths, North to Whippendell Wood and Chandlers Cross; West towards Croxley.

B A hide

C Car park

D Watercress farm, private property

E Grand Union Canal

F River Gade

G The park. For detail of this corner of the park see the map on page 23, or see page 12 for a map of the entire park.

PLACES

Watford station, by the park, is on the Metropolitan Line of the London 'tube'. Locals call it *Watford Met*, the TFL (Transport for London) website calls it *Watford Underground*. Do not confuse it with Watford Junction which is 1.2 miles away. Watford Met. is south of the Park in Cassiobury Park Avenue, a three minute walk from the Park, see page 27.

At the entrance to the park near the station is Cafe Cha Cha (clock tower on the roof and "Cha Cha" above the door), it is open 7 days 10am to 5pm (about 4.30pm in the Winter) including bank holidays (but closed Christmas to new year). Outside are picnic benches and a small children's playground; inside there is also a large room that can be hired for private events such as parties.

The paddling pools are open daily between 10am and 7pm from Good Friday to mid-September. Entrance is free. The refreshments kiosk (in the middle of the photograph) is open all the year round.

The toilets are open Monday 9am to 2.30pm. Tuesday to Friday 8am to 3pm.

But weekends vary: June to about Sep. 8am to 7.30pm; Mid Oct. to about March 9.30am to 4.30pm; other times of year, 8am to 3pm.

Cassiobury is known to families with small children: the big playground, paddling pools, bouncy castle and miniature

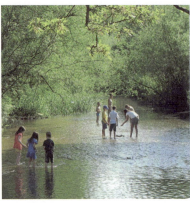

railway. A few yards away are picnic benches and a bridge over the River Gade, the river is wide and shallow, children paddle or fish. A few yards from the river is a weir, then a bridge over the canal and lock where you can watch the boats.

Above left: the river by the bridges at 6.30am, as the ground mist rises. Above right: this picture taken in the Winter, in the summer it's a huge mass of leaves. Below left: the bridge is known, to boaters, as 'that bridge where the children wave". Below right: from the bridge over the canal, looking North.

It is unfashionable to photographs children in paddling pools, so here is a tastefully fuzzy picture of a child playing in a fountain and two general shots of the pools and playground when empty.

Opposite the playground is the station for the miniature railway.

It is customary for small children to come to the park to admire the swans and feed the ducks, this child is feeding the seagulls.

ACTIVITIES

EVENTS

LINKS

FINDING YOUR WAY AROUND THE PARK (see the map of the Park on page 12)

HOW TO GET TO THE PICNIC BENCHES
AT THE BRIDGES BY THE RIVER AND CANAL

Most of my walks start from the picnic benches by the bridges over the river and canal, as shown by the big black arrow on the map below. Also: **A** bridge over the canal. **B** bridge over the river. **C** toilets. **D** level crossing. **E** picnic benches (if you are here, you are at the wrong picnic benches!). **F** tea / ice cream kiosk, paddling pools, changing rooms, toilets. **G** train rides. **H** playground. **I** bouncy castle.

This is a good meeting point. If you are waiting for friends, admire the river, watch the boats go through the lock; if you are accompanied by impatient children, watch the trains, let them paddle in the river, promise them the swings after the walk.

However, unless you live in a hole by the river, you will have a previous 'starting point' at an entrance to the park, or at the car park. The next three pages show every possible route across the park to the picnic benches

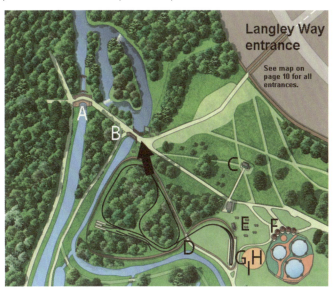

TO THE PICNIC BENCHES BY THE RIVER AND CANAL

FROM THE *LANGLEY WAY* ENTRANCE

NORTH SIDE OF THE PARK IN PARKSIDE DRIVE
SAT NAV. WD17 3BA, 161

mns	DIRECTIONS
0	Take the path between the houses.
3	Arrive at the picnic benches by the bridge over the river.

TO THE PICNIC BENCHES BY THE RIVER AND CANAL

FROM *THE GARDENS* ENTRANCE,
NORTH SIDE OF THE PARK IN PARKSIDE DRIVE
SAT NAV. WD17 3AY, 89

mns	DIRECTIONS
0	Take the passage between the houses and walk into the park.
2	Turn right at the crossroads (past the sign *Cyclists Please Dismount*).
10	Arrive at the picnic benches by the bridge over the river.

TO THE PICNIC BENCHES BY THE RIVER AND CANAL

FROM THE *STRATFORD WAY* ENTRANCE
NORTH SIDE OF THE PARK IN PARKSIDE DRIVE
SAT NAV. WD17 3AU, 41

mns	DIRECTIONS
0	Take the passage between the houses and walk into the park.
2	At the crossroads (by the bin) turn right.
	Keep going, past the paddling pools and playground (to your left).
15	Arrive at the picnic benches by the bridge over the river.

TO THE PICNIC BENCHES BY THE RIVER AND CANAL

FROM THE STATION OR CAR PARK IN THE PARK (SHORTEST ROUTE)
This is Watford *Metropolitan Line* station (London Underground) WD18 7LD, 57

mns	DIRECTIONS
0	Turn left out of the station.
4	Turn right to the park .
5	and into the car park – and walk the entire length of the car park.
	At the end of the car take the path across the grass.
2	At the end turn right (the river will be on your left).
7	Arrive at the picnic benches by the bridge over the river.

TO THE PICNIC BENCHES BY THE RIVER AND CANAL
FROM THE STATION (PRETTIEST ROUTE)

This is Watford *Metropolitan Line* station (London Underground) WD18 7LD, 57

mns	DIRECTIONS
0	Turn right out of the station (past the back of Watford Grammar School for Boys, see picture).
2	At the pedestrian lights turn left into Shepherds Road.
3	and ahead into the park (past the barrier, keep left).
	On your right is a big house (it contains a cafe called Cha Cha), on your left are tennis courts.
4	Turn left at the end.
9	Turn left at the crossroads.
16	You are at the picnic benches, ahead is the bridge over the river.

TO THE PICNIC BENCHES BY THE RIVER AND CANAL
FROM THE *RICKMANSWORTH ROAD*

WEST SIDE OF THE PARK IN PARKSIDE DRIVE, WD17 3AA, 1

Sat Nav postcode for walking only (two minute walk)

mns	DIRECTIONS
0	Two paths go into the park, take the right hand path
19	(could be 18mns, could be 20mns, depends on how fast you walk) Arrive at the picnic benches by the bridge over the river

HOW TO FIND THE PARK FROM THE STATION OR FROM A412 AT THE ASCOT ROAD ROUNDABOUT

WATFORD STATION

The station is Watford *Metropolitan Line* on the London Underground. Locals call it "Watford Met", the TFL (Transport for London) website calls it *Watford Underground*. If your Sat Nav. doesn't show stations, go to WD18 7LD, 57

FROM THE STATION
TO THE SHEPHERDS ROAD ENTRANCE (nearest)

mns	DIRECTIONS (for key see page 9)
0	Turn right out of the station (it doesn't really matter if you cross the road immediately or walk along the station forecourt).
2	At the pedestrian lights turn left into Shepherds Road
3	and ahead into the park (past the barrier, keep left).
4	On your right is a big house (it contains a cafe called Cha Cha), on your left are tennis courts.
4¼	**i** At the main path, left is towards the playground, paddling pools, railway, canal, river and Whippendell Wood, right goes to the Rickmansworth Road (then a ten minute walk to the town centre).

FROM THE STATION
TO THE GADE AVENUE ENTRANCE AND CAR PARK IN THE PARK

mns	DIRECTIONS
0	Turn left out of the station.
	Turn right at the end into the car park (the park is all around you).
	i If you have driven and you park in the middle or far end of the car park, walk to the end (furthest from the entrance), take the path across the grass, turn right at the end, the picnic benches by the river and canal will be on your left, total walk from car park six minutes, OR if you walked, turn left at the entrance to the car park alongside the wall / fence, turn right at the end (stay in the park!), turn right again at the end (keep the river to your left), total walk from car park eight minutes.

FROM A412 RICKMANSWORTH ROAD AT THE ASCOT ROAD ROUNDABOUT, TO THE CAR PARK IN THE PARK OR TO THE STATION

These directions are for walking. If you want to know where to park, see page 10.

mns		DIRECTIONS (for key see page 9)
0		From the junction of A412 Rickmansworth Road / Gade Avenue turn into Gade Avenue and walk along the end of the common to the notice, *Welcome to Cassio Common* (at the end of a footpath). Or from the roundabout, take the footpath across Cassio Common, at the end of the path is Gade Avenue, turn left. Either way, my starting-point (0) is at the junction of the footpath and Gade Avenue, by the notice, *Welcome to Cassio Common.*
		Continue along Gade Avenue, under the high railway bridge and past the pedestrian lights.
	Dtr	Walk across the grass to the bridge and river, admire the view, walk back.
4½		You arrive at a junction.
	i	How you perceive this junction depends on whether you drive. For drivers, the road curves right (and changes name to Swiss Avenue), with a smaller road ahead (still Gade Avenue). For non-drivers you can go ahead (Gade Avenue) or you can go right (Swiss Avenue).
		For the car park in the park, walk on left pavement.
	8½	and continue ahead into the car park in the park.
		Or for the station, stay on the right pavement, follow road to the right
	9	at the end turn right,
	10	and the station will be on your right.
	i	There is no parking in the main road (Rickmansworth Road) and very limited parking in Gade Avenue. If you have a reason to park in this area (e.g. for the Guy Fawkes fireworks display when all approaches to the park are closed) try Watford Business Park on the other side of the roundabout, a 20mn walk from the park. Or see *Parking* on page10.

WALKS IN THE PARK

(See the map of the park on page 12)

This aerial photograph of the park was taken in 1928.

THE PARK, about 50mns

This is my circular walk of the *entire* park. I've started the walk at my favourite corner of the park, by the picnic benches at the bridges over the canal and river, close to the playgrounds, paddling pools and miniature railway (see detailed map on page 23) but you can start anywhere in the park.

➔ The nearest entrance for the picnic benches is the Langley Way entrance (the junction of Parkside Drive and Langley Way), the entrance with the gate marked "Welcome to Cassiobury", Sat. Nav. location is WD17 3BA, 161. From the gate, continue ahead for 3mns, to the picnic benches on your right.

From the picnic benches face the park (with your back to the bridge) and take the path ahead to your right, alongside the wooden fence, heading away from the river. Stay on this path for 4½mns, passing the end of the playground and the station for the miniature railway to your left, then the river will re-appear on to your right.

Take the path that forks left to the car park (for 1mn).
Walk the length of the car park (for 1½mn) and out onto the road. ➔ if you start the walk from here, walk back to the entrance (where you drove in) then out onto the road. Sat. nav. location is WD18 7LB, 2.
Continue ahead (stay on the left pavement) for ½mn then follow the pavement left (the road changes name from Gade Avenue to Cassiobury Park Avenue).
In 3½mns you pass the station on your right.
➔ if you start here, turn right out of the station. Sat. nav. location is WD18 7LD, 57.
2mns from the station are pedestrian lights, turn left into Shepherds Road
and 1mn later, continue ahead into the park
and in another 1mn the path ends (between the tennis courts and the house).
Turn right.

i	The big house. This is Cafe Cha Cha, see page 15 for details.

Stay on this path for 8mns, almost to the main road

✣	This is the A412; to the right it's called Rickmansworth Road, it goes through Rickmansworth and ends at Denham at the A40; to the left it's called St Albans Road, it goes through North Watford, crosses the A41 at *The Dome* roundabout and ends at the A405 North Orbital Road.

then turn sharp left, away from the road, stay in the park.

➜ If you start from here (at the main road) you will notice that there are two paths, take the right hand fork. There is no useable Sat Nav postcode.

> ℹ If (facing the road from the park) you were to turn left into the road then take first left, the first house is at **WD17 3AA, 1** - this is the nearest sat. nav. location but there is no access by car from the main road (some sat navs can be set to 'walking' mode but will take you on a 20 minute walk around Watford to get to the sat nav location ten yards away.

> ℹ If you turn left into the main road, the Peace Hospice and the Colosseum are on your left, then you can follow the pavement left and either continue ahead for the library and The Horns pub, or double-back under the underpass. From the Park to the underpass is a four minute walk, and on the other side of the underpass is Watford High Street - Watford Town Centre really is that close to the Park! The entire High Street is pedestrianised, see top of next page for details.

After 6mns you are at a crossroads of paths, continue ahead (to your right is the entrance to the park at Parkside Drive / Stratford Way).

➜ if you start from this entrance, take the passage between the houses and walk into the park, and at the crossroads (by the bin) turn right. Sat. nav. location **is** WD17 3AU, 41.

After 4mns you are at a crossroads of paths, to your right is the entrance to the park at Parkside Drive / The Gardens.

➜ if you start from this entrance: take the passage between the houses and walk into the park and turn right at the crossroads (past the sign *Cyclists Please Dismount*) . Sat. nav. location is WD17 3AY, 89.

After another 7mns you arrive at the picnic benches by the bridges over the river and canal, see my first direction.

- if you started at the junction of Parkside Drive and Langley Way (the gate marked *Welcome to Cassiobury Park)*, turn right (with the remaining picnic benches on your left), through the trees, 2mns to the exit.

➜ if you start from here (junction of Parkshide Drive and Langley Way) sat. nav. location is WD17 3BS.

THE HIGH STREET

The Park is a 4mn walk from the underpass at the 'top' of Watford High street, the end of the High Street with the ponds and benches and walkways (rebuilt in 2013).

From the underpass until you pass under a road bridge takes another 4mns. This part of town is known for its night clubs, it is the clubbing centre of South Hertfordshire.

From passing under the bridge to Clarendon Road, on your left, is a 1mn walk (turn left here for the Palace Theatre, a few yards on your right).

Continue along the High Street (past the town centre bus stops) and in 1½mns you pass a passage on your left leading to Charter Place. At the end of the passage turn left for Watford Market (will move / has moved in Spring 2014) or right for the Harlequin Shopping Centre (re-branded *intu* in 2013 but still known to locals as *The Harlequin*).

In another 1½mns St Mary's Church is on your right (pretty courtyard, sculptures and benches). Then it's 1½mns to the far entrance (main entrance) of the Harlequin. This end of town is branded *Metro*, with cafes and restaurants for those who want to keep way from the clubs.

The pedestrianized area ends in another 2mns when you get to a main road (the ring road), look diagonally across the road junction, you can see Watford High Street station. Just past the station is Watford Museum.

CIRCULAR WALK OF THE PARK
About 45 minutes

mns	DIRECTIONS
	Start at the picnic benches by the river and canal (see page 23). With your back to the bridge, take the path ahead.
2	The path curves left, the playground will be on your right (see picture) followed by the paddling pools.

	Walk along the avenue of trees.
9	At the crossroads, turn right.
22	At the end (by the main road) turn sharp left, stay in the park.
29	Continue ahead at the crossroads (the exit to the right is onto Parkside Drive at to Stratford Way).
33	Continue ahead at the crossroads at the earth path (the exit diagonally to the right, by the white-roofed hut, comes out onto Parkside Drive at The Gardens).
34	Continue ahead at the main crossroads (same white-roofed hut is to your right).
39	Turn left at the railings, to the paddling pool and alongside the playground.
41	Turn right (double back on yourself), the end of the miniature railway will be on your right, they you will cross a level crossing.
43	At the end, turn right.
44	The picnic benches and bridge will be on your left.

CIRCULAR WALK OF THE PARK
from the station   About 30 minutes

mns	DIRECTIONS
0	Turn right out of the station.
2	At the pedestrian lights turn left into Shepherds Road.
3	and ahead into the park (past the barrier, keep left). On your right is café Cha Cha (the big house), on your left are tennis courts.
4	Turn left at the end.
9	Turn left at the crossroads (ahead would take you out of the park to Parkside Drive at The Gardens).
16	You are at the picnic benches, ahead is the bridge over the river, turn left alongside the wooden fence.
20	Fork left towards the car park, then walk the length of the car park
23	and out onto the road.
24	Turn left into Cassiobury Park Avenue.
28	The station is on your right.

CIRCULAR WALK OF THE PARK
from the car park in the park, about 1 hour

mns	DIRECTIONS
	At the far end of the car park from where you drove in, take the path across the grass. Or if you are on foot and haven't parked in the car park, you don't *have* to walk along the middle of the car park, you can follow my alternative route below, and add 2 minutes to my times.
1	At the end turn right (river on your left, playground on your right).
3½	Keep left past playground (river still on your left).
4½	and over the miniature railway's level crossing.
7	At the crossroads turn right.
16	At the crossroads, turn right.
29	At the end (by the main road) turn sharp left, stay in the park.
36	Continue ahead (the exit to the right is onto Parkside Drive at to Stratford Way).
40	At the crossroads with the earth path continue ahead (the exit to the right, by the white-roofed hut, comes out onto Parkside Drive at The Gardens).
41	Continue ahead at the main crossroads (same white-roofed hut to the right).
46	Turn left at the railings, to the paddling pool and alongside the playground.
47	Turn right (double back on yourself), the end of the miniature railway will be on your right.
49	Across the miniature railway's level crossing.
50	At the end, turn right (or left if you parked in the car park in the park).
57	Car park on left (if you turned left).

Alternative		
		At the entrance to the car park is a wall by the side of a house followed by a long garden fence. Walk along the wall / fence (it should be to your left) towards the woodland.
	1	Turn right at the sign, *Cassiobury Park Local Nature Reserve*.
	2	Turn right at the end.
	4	You are at "1" above, continue ahead.

CIRCULAR WALK OF THE PARK
from Café Cha Cha (by the Shepherds Road entrance near the station)
About 40 minutes

mns		DIRECTIONS (for key see page 9)
mns		Start in the park at Café Cha Cha.
0		Walk so that the front entrance of Cha Cha (and then the little playground) is to your right.
	Dtr	In 30 seconds, look along path to your left, see the tree? It looks like an owl. Have a closer look, see the carvings of animals. Then walk back.
7½		When you get to the main road, turn left (i.e. stay in the park).
(15)	↺	Shortcut back to Cha Cha (2mns), at the first crossroads turn left (path with street lights), past The Owl Tree, at the end of the path you will see Cha Cha ahead to your right.
23		Past the paddling pools, the path bends right, past the picnic benches on your left.
	↺	If you know the park: I'm taking you off to the right, then left onto the path over the level crossing, then the station to the miniature railway will be on your left. But feel free to cut the corner off – go left alongside the paddling pools and playground, the station to the miniature railway will be on your right. Then turn left.
26		At the crossroads turn left, so that you are walking with the wooden fence to your right (see the picture at the bottom of page 30).

At any point between coming out of the trees and reaching the little bridge over the river, turn left and cut across the grass (no path) uphill to the flat-topped tree. This is the high point of the park and a good place to get your bearings, on the next page is my guide to the view.	
9 approx.	Arrive at the tree.

	When you have finished admiring the view, face uphill, stand with your back to tree bench and walk exactly ahead. If you're not sure what 'ahead' is, veer slightly to your right rather than to your left.
29	Turn right onto the path.
32	Turn right onto the path then right at the crossroads.
36	Café Cha Cha will be on your right.

THE VIEW

Sit on the tree bench so that you facing the bottom of the hill, from where you came. You are sitting by the tree to the right of "B" on the map on page 12.

Exactly ahead of you is a bridge over the River Gade, and the bridge is Meadow bridge. Most of the trees are part of the *Cassiobury Park Local Nature Reserve*, but if you look to your right, into the far distance, you will notice a ridge of trees high up, this is the edge of Whippendell Wood.

Ahead to your left, just to the right of the car park, you should see (except in high summer when the leaves are at their thickest) a path disappearing into the distance. This goes to Gade Avenue, ending at the Rickmansworth Road by the double roundabout near Croxley (by the entrance to the business parks), and the Rickmansworth Road runs parallel to the park to your far left, all the way to the other end of the Park behind you.

To your far left (slightly behind you) across the fields is a low pitched-roof building, this is at the bowling green, and as you see from the map on page 12 (obscured by trees from where you sit) it's next to the tennis and squash courts, which is next to Café Cha Cha by the Shepherds Road entrance – so you could take a short cut across the grass, a five minute walk to Cha Cha rather than the ten minute walk listed above.

NINE BRIDGES, 30mns or 45mns
See the map of the nature reserve on page 14

mns	DIRECTIONS (for key see page 9)
0	Start at the picnic benches by the river and canal (see page 23). Face the park (with your back to the bridge) and take the path ahead to your right, alongside the wooden fence, heading away from the river.
2	Over the level crossing. Then the playground will be to your left.
4	Turn right across the bridge over the river and follow the path ahead.
ff	If, at this point, all you can see is water, you will have to turn back. Look at the map on page 14. Pretend to join up points 3-B-6-4. Within this area are 'flood meadows', they flood, they soak up water, they stop the river swelling and flooding Rickmansworth downstream.
8	Cross the small bridge and turn left onto the path.
10	Cross the bridge with the wooden railings
11	and across the narrow bridge with the green metal railings
	and turn right, alongside the river. It looks like a dead end but after 10 paces you can see the path to your left. After another 100 paces the path turns away from the river, but you can see (ahead / to your right) a tree growing out across the water (see the picture on page 57). Walk round this tree (or under the branch if you're *very* short) and you will see that the path continues alongside the river.
14	Turn right across the bridge
15	and continue ahead over the small bridge
17	At the end turn right onto the single-track road
18	and across bridge over the canal
	and on the other side of the bridge turn sharp right, down the steps onto the canal path.
	A blue sign reads, *Cassiobury Park ¼*. You should be walking along the canal path so that the canal is to your right.
31	Cross the bridge at the lock (you can fork left up the gentle slope, 100 yards before the bridge or walk under the bridge to the lock and up the steep slope).
32	and continue ahead to the second bridge, and cross the river to finish

	the walk at the picnic benches where you started.
↺	**Or** just *before* the second bridge turn right (river will be on your left), you can probably still see the canal through the trees to your right, and after 150 paces you will be walking by the side of the canal again.
33	Now keep looking to your left, and turn left exactly by the wooden post that reads *Look out for Kingfishers* (if you get to a bench on your left, you've gone too far). A little river will still be on your left and you will be walking away from the canal.
36	Cross the wooden bridge.
39	Cross the bridge into the park.
	- turn left to return to the picnic benches where you started (keep left at the playground, keep by the river, then over the level crossing, under the big trees, and at the junction of paths you will see the picnic benches) - or turn right if you parked in the car park, which you will see ahead to your left
44	Arrive at picnic benches.

RIVERSIDE AND BACK THROUGH PARK
About 20mns

mns	DIRECTIONS (for key see page 9)
0	Start at the picnic benches by the river and canal (see page 23), cross the bridge
¼	and immediately turn left, so that the river is to your left
	i In the winter and spring you will see the river to your left, in the summer and autumn the willow planted along the riverbank (to stop erosion) will be tall and green and you won't see the river.
	past a *hide* on your left, and over two bridges
8½	turning left immediately after the second bridge (at the crossroads).
	Keep left, keeping the river to your left (you will see the car park to your right, you will pass the end of the playground)
18	then you are back at the picnic benches by the bridge over the river.

THE 'DRY' PATH BY THE RIVER AND THROUGH THE WOODS OF THE NATURE RESERVE, about 20 minutes

Good paths, no mud, and it's flat. However, in the floods of 2012 the surrounding meadows turned into lakes and a new river flowed across one of the paths.

mns	DIRECTIONS (for key see page 9)
0	Start at the picnic benches by the river and canal (see page 23). Cross the bridge
¼	and immediately turn left, onto the path, so that you are walking with the river to your left then the canal to your right.
	ff In the summer you can't see the river and canal at first, because of 'tall reeds'. It is not 'tall reeds'. It is 'spilings', a method of preventing erosion, in this case it's willow, it grows tall in the summer, it's cut back to a few inches in the winter, what you see depends on the time of year.

	Continue ahead over two bridges, and as you leave the second bridge there is a crossroads,
8½	turn left
	Keep left (with the river to your left). You will see the car park to your right, you will pass the end of the playground then the station for the miniature railway then you will cross the level crossing,
18	and then you are back at the picnic benches.

WHIPPENDELLWOODS PICNIC BENCH, about 25mns
SO simple, no map required, I promise!

mns	DIRECTIONS
0	Start at the picnic benches by the river and canal (see page 23), take the bridge over the river then the bridge over the canal and continue ahead for 10 paces.
2	then turn right signposted *PUBLIC FOOTPATH 30*
	Beware of balls as you cross the golf course (look left).
12½	You are at the entrance to Whippendell Wood, the path splays out in four directions, picnic bench to your left.

From the picnic bench you usually see people walking dogs or toddlers, or riding horses or bicycles, or just walking. Here is the unusual sight of someone riding a quad bike at high speed along the bridle path – strictly forbidden I'm sure!

	Have rest. Then walk back.	
25	Arrive at the lock	...you could sit by the lock and watch the boats
	And cross the bridge over the canal	...or watch the boats from the bridge.
	then continue ahead to the bridge over the river	...you could take a detour to the weir on your left
26	And over the bridge	...you have small children, play poo-sticks...or if it's hot, they can go paddling.
26½	To the picnic benches where you started	...a picnic?

STROLLS IN THE PARK

(See the map of the park on page 12)

In this section I assume you want a casual slow stroll rather than a 'walk'. The numbers in the left column are minutes and allow for this slow pace. Each walk starts and finishes at an entrance to the park, or the car park.

FROM THE CAR PARK IN THE PARK, 6 minutes

0	From the far end of the car park (from where you drove in) (if you drove) take the footpath across the open grass.
1	At the end turn right.
	In your 5mn walk you pass many landmarks: the river is on your left, there's a bench, a mini-wier and a footbridge, a playground (and, in the summer, a bouncy castle), a miniature railway and a level crossing.
6	The picnic benches.

FROM THE LANGLEY ROAD ENTRANCE, 8mns

0	Start at the entrance on Parkside Drive, at the junction of Langley Road. This is the entrance with the gate marked *Welcome to Cassiobury Park*. At the end of the patch into the park (by the sign with the map) continue for about 50 paces.
1¼	And just before the bin (before the bench) turn right across the grass, towards the trees.
3	On the other side of the trees the path is clearer, it goes (to your right) to the sign that reads *Cassiobury Park Local Nature Reserve*, but you must turn <u>left</u> onto the path, towards the picnic benches.
4	At the picnic benches turn sharp left onto the path.
	In the winter you will see, in the distance, the backs of houses at the road where you started; in the summer you will be walking under the branches of large trees.
8	You are back at the gate where you started.

FROM THE LANGLEY ROAD ENTRANCE, 10mns

0	Take the wide path between the houses (at the gate, *Welcome to Cassiobury*) to the sign with the map, then keep going for 50 paces.
1¼	and turn right, across the grass, before the bin (and before the bench). On the other side of the trees the path is clearer, you can see (to your right) a sign, *Cassiobury Park Local Nature Reserve*,
3	but you must turn LEFT, towards the picnic benches
4	and *at* the picnic benches turn sharp left
7½	back to the gate at Parkside Drive.

FROM THE LANGLEY ROAD ENTRANCE, 10mns

with options to extend the round trip by 1mn, 2mn, 3mn, 4mn or 18mns

0	Start at the entrance on Parkside Drive, at the junction of Langley Road. This is the entrance with the gate marked *Welcome to Cassiobury Park*.
1	Turn left past the bench, towards the hexagonal-roofed huts (they're the changing rooms for the paddling pools). Info: half way along this path, the big hut to the right is a public toilet.
3½	At the end turn right.
6½	At the crossroads at the picnic benches, turn right.*
10	You are back to the gate where you started.
	* alternatively, you could take a detour of 30 seconds to go onto the bridge and look at the river, and maybe continue another 30 seconds to the weir on the right and maybe continue another 30 seconds to the bridge over the canal and maybe walk down to the lock (another 30 seconds) and maybe continue along the canal (with the canal to your right) to a bench, 9mns walking *really* slowly.

FROM THE LANGLEY ROAD ENTRANCE

12mns, with options to extend the round trip by 1mn, 2mn, 3mn, 4mn,18mns

0		Start at the entrance on Parkside Drive, at the junction of Langley Road. This is the entrance with the gate marked *Welcome to Cassiobury Park*.
1		Turn left past the bench, towards the hexagonal-roofed huts (they're the changing rooms for the paddling pools).
	i	Half way along this path, the big hut to the right is a public toilet, see page 15 for opening times.
3½		At the end turn left.
4		Then turn right. The picnic benches at the paddling pools will be to your right, then the playground will be to your left and the miniature railway to your right.
5		Follow the fence to your right, round the end of the miniature railway.
8		At the junction of paths, bear right, past three picnic benches.
		In the winter you will see, in the distance, the backs of houses at the road where you started; in the summer you will be walking under the branches of large trees.
12		You are back at the gate where you started.
	Dtr	or you could take a detour of 30 seconds to go onto the bridge and look at the river
	Dtr	… and then maybe continue for another 30 seconds to look at the weir on the right
	Dtr	… and then maybe continue for another 30 seconds to the bridge over the canal
	Dtr	…and then maybe walk down to the lock (another 30 seconds)
	Dtr	…and then maybe continue along the canal (which should be to your right) to a bench (another 5 minutes).

FURTHER AFIELD

If you visit the park regularly and know all the paths in the main park (see the map on page 12), or if you consider paths across neatly cut grass and under freshly-trimmed trees 'boring' – then you are ready to travel further afield.

The maps on the following pages are open source maps,
© OpenStreetMap contributors, see www.openstreetmap.org

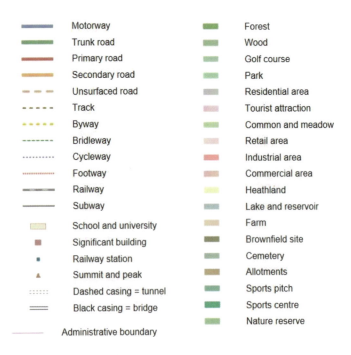

—	Motorway
—	Trunk road
—	Primary road
—	Secondary road
– – –	Unsurfaced road
- - - -	Track
· · · · ·	Byway
- - - - - -	Bridleway
··········	Cycleway
············	Footway
━━━	Railway
━━━	Subway
▪	School and university
■	Significant building
•	Railway station
▲	Summit and peak
:::::::	Dashed casing = tunnel
===	Black casing = bridge
——	Administrative boundary
▪	Forest
▪	Wood
▪	Golf course
▪	Park
▪	Residential area
▪	Tourist attraction
▪	Common and meadow
▪	Retail area
▪	Industrial area
▪	Commercial area
▪	Heathland
▪	Lake and reservoir
▪	Farm
▪	Brownfield site
▪	Cemetery
▪	Allotments
▪	Sports pitch
▪	Sports centre
▪	Nature reserve

GOLF COURSE, WHIPPENDELLWOODS AND CANAL
About 50 minutes

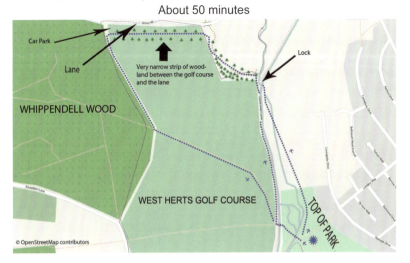

The path into the woodland starts by the canal 15mns North of the park. There are two ways to get here: either along the canal path, or through the wetland nature reserve and across the canal by walking over the canal gate (because there is no bridge). Either way is about 50 minutes.

ROUTE 1, through the wetland nature reserve, providing it's not flooded.	
mns	**DIRECTIONS** (for key see page 9)
	Start at the picnic benches by the river and canal (see page 23), walk along the grass (not the path) keeping the river to your left
	to the sign *Cassiobury Park Local Nature Reserve*
1½	And take the path ahead (river still to your left, but now hidden by woodland).
3½	Turn left at the bench (ahead is just a dead end that finishes at a playing field).
	The AstroTurf hockey pitches are used by Watford Grammar School for Boys and West Herts Hockey Club; the rugby pitches on either side are used by the school and the Fullerians; this is also the home of *Sun*

	Postal Sports FC (which was founded in 1898).
	Eventually the canal will be visible on your left.
	The path ends abruptly at a playing field, by another sign *Cassiobury Park Local Nature Reserve*.
13	Turn left.
14	At the trees turn left to the lock. The path ends here, completely. The only way to cross the canal is by walking over the canal gate, holding onto the rail.
14¼	Turn left so that you are walking with the canal to your left.
15	The path becomes a bridge, with water to your right (in a dry season it looks like a big pond, in a wet season it looks like a river).
	At the end of the white rail, turn right onto the path into the woodland.
	Continue at "Both routes".

ROUTE 2, the simple route, along the canal path	
	Start at the picnic benches by the river and canal (see page 23), cross the river, continue ahead and cross the canal
	and turn right on the other side of the bridge (so that you are walking along the canal path with the canal to your right).
11	Ahead you can see that the canal bends 90° right and on the curve is a 'bridge' formed by a brick wall on the right and a metal fence on the left (see photograph on page 88).
11½	*Immediately* before that metal fence to your left, turn left onto the footpath up into the woods.
	Continue at "Both routes".

BOTH ROUTES		
R1	R2	
15	11½	You have taken the path into the woodland.
16		The path forks, it really doesn't matter which fork you take.
		You will find yourself going steadily uphill, you can't get lost, you are walking along a narrow strip of woodland, with open fields to your right and West Herts Golf Course to your left.
23		You may hear cars, there's a lane to the right (Grove Mill Lane).
28	25	At the top the ground levels (you are definitely not going uphill any more), there's a slight clearing, and the path disappears. Continue ahead, there are only two possible outcomes: - you come to a wide track (if you look right you can see a the barrier to a car park).
30		Turn left onto the track.
		or
		- you come to the car park (or possibly woodstacks by the side of the car park), walk along (or round) the car park to the barrier by the wide track. Other landmarks: a map of the woodland and a sign that reads, *Horses must keep to perimeter track*.
30		With your back to the barrier, walk along the track. You should be walking very slightly uphill, if you're going steeply downhill, turn back.
36	34	Follow the track left past a picnic bench and a sign to Cassiobury Park.
		ff Careful as you cross the golf course, look right. If a golfer drives a ball towards you without noticing, he will scream "Fore!!". Your response should *not* be to face the direction of the shout, but to bend down and cover your head with your arms, in anticipation of being struck by a golf ball.
48	46½	Bridge to your left. cross the canal (or walk down to the lock to watch the boats)
49	48	and over the bridge over the river
½	48½	The picnic benches.

TWO WALKS FROM THE A412 RICKMANSWORTH ROAD AT ASCOT ROAD NEAR CROXLEY AND THE BUSINESS PARKS AROUND THE SOUTHERN END OF THE NATURE RESERVE

This map shows the roads and paths from the station and car park in the park, to the southern tip of the nature reserve. See page 14 for a map of the nature reserve.

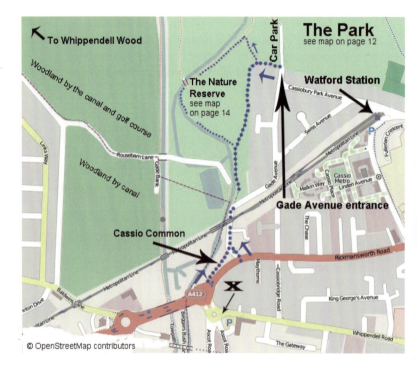

For the sake of these two walks please ignore the "x", it marks the exact point the photograph on page 58 was taken (for the *Common Moor, Croxley* walk), with camera facing south.

NATURE RESERVE SOUTH, FROM CASSIO COMMON* (40mns)

* at the junction of Gade Avenue and A412 Rickmansworth Road

OR FROM THE CAR PARK IN THE PARK (30 mns)

(The next walk is similar, but 10 minutes shorter)

See the route marked in heavier dots on the map on page 50.

mns	DIRECTIONS (for key see page 9)
	From the Junction of A412 Rickmansworth Road and Gade Avenue, walk along Gade Avenue to the path on your left and the sign that reads *Welcome to Cassio* Common. This is your starting point. Or if you start at big roundabout in the main road, cut across the common and turn left into Gade Avenue (same starting point).
0	Continue along Gade Avenue (heading away from the main road)
1	to the bridge and pedestrian lights
1½	and at the second pedestrian light fork left onto the footpath
	and cross the bridge.
2	On the other side of the bridge, turn right onto the path (no choice).
	Continue at "11" below. Deduct (approx.) 10mns from the times.
0	Start at the entrance to the car park, where you drove in over the ramp (if you drove). Face the NO EXIT sign (with your back to the car park) and turn right onto the path, past the bench.
	At the end (after just 30 paces) turn right, towards the woodland.
1	Turn left at the sign *Cassiobury Park Local Nature Reserve.* Woodland will be to your right, railings will be to your left.
4½	At the river, turn left (so that the river is to your right).
7½	Just before the road, turn right over the bridge (then right onto the path - no choice).
11	At the lamppost by the locked gate on your left (unlikely to be open!) turn right (woodland now on both sides).
	ℹ️ After very heavy rain the first few yards of this path will be flooded, retrace your steps until you can see not-so-wet woodland, and cut the corner.
	Over a small bridge then over a larger bridge (over the river).
13	Then turn left.
15	At the river, continue ahead over the bridge (then over a smaller bridge).

	You will find yourself walking along the canal and, eventually, you will see the river to your right (though in the summer the river will be obscured by willow).
24	Turn right over the bridge to the picnic benches (or detour left to visit the weir and the canal...then come back)
24½	and turn right (wooden fence to your right).
	You cross the level crossing for the miniature railway then the end of the playground, then you will see the car park ahead to your left.
29	**Either** Fork left to the car park
	or to continue to Gade Avenue, like this:
30	Keep right, keep the river to your right.
33	At the bridge continue ahead, alongside the river (looks like a dead end but after 10 yards you can see the path ahead, curving left).
	After 100 paces the path turns away from the river, but you can see (ahead to your right) a tree growing out across the water. Walk round this tree and you will see that the path continues alongside the river. Stay on this path, along the riverbank.
36	Past the bridge, keep right, keep the river to your right.
40	At the end turn right onto the road (Gade Avenue).

Where you go from now depends on where you live / have parked / are catching the bus. In 90 seconds you will be at the path across Cassio Common then it's another 90 second walk to the main road at the roundabout (A412 / Rickmansworth Road), or the same main road directly ahead is a 30 second walk.

NATURE RESERVE SOUTH, FROM CASSIO COMMON* (30mns)

* at the junction of Gade Avenue and A412 Rickmansworth Road.

OR FROM THE CAR PARK IN THE PARK (20 mns)

(The previous walk is similar, but 10 minutes longer)

See the route marked in lighter dots on the map on page 50.

mns	DIRECTIONS (for key see page 9)
	From the Junction of A412 Rickmansworth Road and Gade Avenue, walk along Gade Avenue to the path on your left and the sign that reads *Welcome to Cassio* Common. This is your starting point. Or if you start at big roundabout in the main road, cut across the common and turn left into Gade Avenue, this is your starting point.
0	Continue along Gade Avenue
1	to the bridge and pedestrian light
1½	and at the second pedestrian light fork left onto the footpath (do not cross the bridge).
2	and turn left onto the concrete path. You should be walking with the river to your left.
.	***ff*** It often looks as if they are cutting down all the trees in the woodland to the right. They are not 'cutting down all the trees', they are thinning the woodland, so that more light enters, there is growth from the ground, this encourages greater diversity of plants and wildlife…and in 20 years (if they leave it alone) it will all have grown back again.
4½	At the crossroads there's a bridge to your left – ignore it, continue ahead. Now continue at "7" on the next page.
	ff If you had started at the car park you would have approached from the right. And it's just coincidence that, to this point, is 4½ minutes either way. So the times for the remainder of the walk are the same.
0	Start at the entrance to the car park, where you drove in (if you drove) over the ramp. Face the *NO EXIT* sign, turn right onto the path, past the bench.
	At the end (after just 30 paces) turn right, towards the woodland.
1	Turn left at the sign *Cassiobury Park Local Nature Reserve*. Woodland will be to your right, railings will be to your left.
4½	At the crossroads at the bridge over the river (see picture) turn right so that you are walking with the river to your left.

7	At the river continue ahead over the bridge.
	You are going to turn right onto a narrow footpath, it's not easy to find, your landmarks are: a wooden *hide* on the right, a red rubbish bin on the left, and you will now be walking alongside the canal...
13	...then a post marked "Look out for Kingfishers" (it's meant to be a nature trail notice, not a warning). This is where you turn right onto the path. If you get to the next bench on your left, you have gone 50 paces too far, if you can no longer see the canal on your left, you have gone 1 minute too far.
	You will find yourself walking alongside a small river to your left, more of a 'trickle' in times of drought, or if the season is very wet you will see an awful lot of water.
18	Cross the bridge into the park and turn right, you will see the car park

	ahead of you to the left
19	and fork left
20	to the car park
	or
	to get back to Gade Avenue / Cassio Common, go through the car park
0	and out onto the main road.
	Ahead at the junction (if in doubt, stay on the right hand side of the road)
	past the pedestrian lights / under the railway bridge
8½	to Cassio Common.

COMMON MOOR, CROXLEY
About 2 hours, 20 minutes

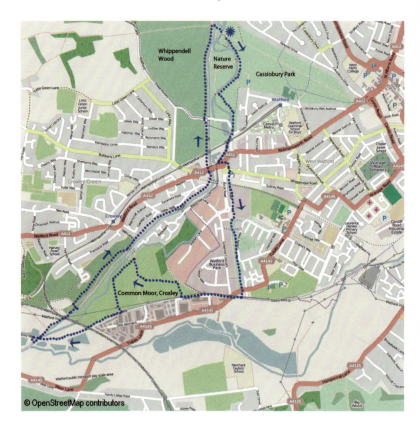

mns	**DIRECTIONS** (for key see page 9)
0	Start at the picnic benches by the river and canal (see page 23), face the park (with your back to the bridge) and take the path ahead to your right, alongside the wooden fence, heading away from the river (see the photograph at the bottom of page 30).
2½	The swings will be on your left, then the river will be to your right.
6	The path forks, left towards car park or right alongside the river – stay to the right, alongside the river, and the same at the next junction, keep right, so that the river is to your right.
9	At the bridge continue ahead towards the riverbank, it looks like a dead end but after 7 paces you can see the path ahead, curving left – follow the path.
	After 100 paces the path turns away from the river, but you can see (ahead to your right) a tree growing out across the water. Walk round this tree (or under the branch if you're very short) and you will see that the path continues alongside the river.

12½	Past the bridge, keep right, keep the river to your right.
15½	At the end turn right onto Gade Avenue, under the railway bridge.

17½	and turn right onto the path across the common (by the sign *Welcome to Cassio Common*).
19	Cross the main road (A412 / Rickmansworth Road) at the traffic island before the roundabout and turn right onto the pavement, then follow the pavement to the left.
	ff By 2016 there will be a new station here, Ascot Road (London Transport Metropolitan Line), it will be behind the clock tower in the photograph (by 2016 this junction will look quite different).
20	Now you can see a second roundabout (marked 'Croxley') and if you look ahead you can see (from left to right) "Big Yellow Self Storage", a low railway bridge, a clock tower and a dual carriageway. Keep an eye on the low railway bridge, the photo below was taken from "X" on the map on page 50, facing south.

21	cross the road (Whippendell Road)
23	and under the low railway bridge.
26½	The road runs out, continue ahead through the concrete posts (in 2013 it was by a garage called *Steven Eagel*)
27½	and fork right onto the path signed, *Ebury Way ½*.
	The path curves left, trees on right, industrial buildings (Watford Business Park) behind a wall to your right. To your left is open space by a housing estate (with the public exercise machines).
	Cross the road (Tolpits Lane), continue along the path for 100 paces
36½	and turn right onto Ebury Way signed, *Rickmansworth 2½*.

	ff	Behind the mesh fences, Royal Mail is to your right (people collecting parcels have difficulty finding it); to your left is Camelot (National Lottery).

42	The footpath (Ebury Way) joins the road. After 20 paces take the path to the right, through the hedge, to the sign *Croxley Common Moor* - go through the gate onto the moor, taking the path ahead, keeping to the line of trees to your right. 

45	Fork left towards the centre of the moor (about when you are level with the gate in the trees to your right) and aim for the gap in the trees in the distance, which you will see quite clearly as you get closer.
49	On the other side of the gap in the trees you are back on the moor, continue ahead, after a couple of hundred yards you are high enough to see the other side of the moor, you are aiming for a river just to the left of the houses.
53	At the river turn left along the river bank. The river should be to your right. Trouble with weather? Trouble with small children? You could cut the walk short here (35mns back to park).
	↺ Go *through* the gate, over the bridge, over the second bridge (over the canal), and down onto the canal path. Walk with the canal to your right. In 25mns you will be at the next lock, 3mns later is Bridge 168, cross it, and on the other side fork left onto the footpath into the woods; across two footbridges and continue ahead; the path ends in the park within sight of the car park, or keep left for the picnic benches by the river.
59½	At the wooden bench, turn left to cut across the common. The path isn't clear, but it doesn't matter, just aim for the pylon. Walk carefully, if the season has been wet, there will be cool clear water between the tufts.

	ff	According to the O.S. map you could continue along the river all the way to the railway bridge then turn left to a gate. In the drought of 2011. I tried this and found myself walking ankle-deep in water, then by the spring of 2013 (following a year of rain) it was a lake.
1:02½	At the pylon, take the short path towards the transmitting tower (if you find your way blocked by a stream, move a few yards to your left, then you can cross), then through the gate and turn right.	
1:15	Turn right onto the canal path (do this by turning left immediately after the bridge, down the steps, then under the bridge).	
1:17	to the lock.	
1:20	Immediately after the bridge is a footpath that climbs up into woodland.	
1:22	At the bench, follow the path to the right.	
1:32	A clearing, benches, a view over the canal and Common.	
	At the end of the clearing is a steep path back down to the canal at a lock (Common Moor Lock).	
	↺	Emergency Escape Route. By lock, take the path signed *Croxley Station*. Walk uphill for 2mns to the main road (and look back at the view!). You will see the station ahead, it's on the other side of the road, cross carefully. The walk from the canal to the station is less than 4 minutes; the journey from the canal to the picnic benches will be probably be 5 or 10 minutes quicker than walking, but it depends on how long you have to wait for a train.
	You should now be walking along the canal path, with the canal to your right.	
2:05	You are back at Bridge 68	
	↺	If you parked in the car park in the park, there is a shortcut from here: cross the canal at bridge 168; on the other side fork left onto the footpath into the woods; across two footbridges and continue ahead; the path ends in the park within sight of the car park.
2:20	Cross the bridge over the canal (you can do this by walking up the long slope, or by continuing under the bridge and up the short steep slope on the other side) then continue ahead, past the weir, over the bridge over the river	
2:22	to the picnic benches where you started.	

TWO WALKS ROUND WHIPPENDELL WOOD

WHIPPENDELL WOOD, SHORT LOOP, about 35mns

See the route marked in lighter dots on the map

mns	DIRECTIONS
0	Start at the picnic benches by the river and canal (see page 23). Cross over the bridge over the river, then ahead and over the bridge over the canal.
1½	Take the footpath ahead, up the steep hill, *PUBLIC FOOTPATH 31*.
	Continue ahead on the footpath (take care to continue exactly ahead, each time you cross the golf course).

	3	Through the band of trees and across the golf course (look left)
	4	and back into the trees
	7½	and across golf course (look right) – it *is* a public footpath, the golfers *will* stop playing to let you cross.
	10	At the bottom of the hill turn right (mud warning)
13	At the bottom of the hill, at the crossroads of paths, continue ahead (overgrown in the summer) for 10 yards	
	i	If you have just encountered a lot of mud, the following 100 yards will be even muddier. Alternative route, continue ahead for another 10 yards (overgrown in summer), turn right onto the lane, turn right at the gate back onto the path (left onto the path please).
15	and fork right (to the *right* of the HORSES sign).	

22	At the end turn right onto the track (picnic bench on right).
32	Turn left across the bridge over the canal, then ahead over the bridge across the river.
34	Picnic benches on left.

WHIPPENDELL WOOD, LONG LOOP, about 1hr 40mns

See the route marked in heavier dots on the map on page 61.

mns	DIRECTIONS (for key see page 9)
0	Start at the picnic benches by the river and canal (see page 23), take the bridge over the river then the bridge over the canal and ahead up the steep hill, signposted *Whippendell Woods ½ mile / Public Footpath 31 leading to Rosebaum Lane*.
	Continue ahead, the path crosses two open expanses of golf course; the second time, you walk across the middle of a beautifully manicured green, this *is* a public footpath goes, just continue ahead, the footpath continues on the other side of the green (but do stop, look, give way to fast-moving golf balls.
13	And ahead into the woodland (Whippendell wood), down the steep hill.
16	At the bottom of the hill turn right (mud warning).
	_i If you have just encountered a lot of mud, the following 100 yards will be even muddier. Alternative route, continue ahead for another 10 yards (overgrown in summer), turn right onto the lane, turn right at the gate back onto the path (left onto the path please).
	At the gate continue ahead and fork left up the hill. Then the path goes downhill (wooden 'steps').
40	At the very end (the *very* end, past the *No Horses* sign) turn right, up the hill.
43	Landmark: you will see, through the trees on your left, caravans and greenhouses, these are the 'greenhouses' marked on the maps that mark the circular walk.
55	At the junction of paths keep left, alongside the wire fence (there's a pit to your right).
	The wire fence eventually runs out (it turns left 90°) – continue exactly ahead, don't worry about the path, just aim aim for the car park (you should see *some* cars through the trees).
1:05	Then turn right alongside the car park.
	At the top of the hill at the end of the car park, turn right onto the track signed *Horse riders must keep to the perimeter track*.
1:25	Follow the track to the left, by the picnic bench, signed *Public Footpath 30 to Cassiobury Park*.
1.37	Cross the bridges to to the picnic benches.

WHIPPENDELL WOODS, CHANDLERS CROSS
AND THE SHORT WAY BACK, ACROSS THE GOLF COURSE
About 1hr 20mn

mns	DIRECTIONS (for key see page 9)
	Start at the picnic benches by the river and canal (see page 23), cross the bridge over the river then cross the bridge over the canal, and continue ahead for 10 paces.
2	then turn right signposted *PUBLIC FOOTPATH 30*.
13	There's a picnic bench on your left and a choice of three paths. Take path ahead, passing to the right of the map, steeply downhill.
A summary of the route from here is stunningly simple: continue ahead over the lane, turn left immediately after the barn, continue ahead at every choice, and in about an hour you'll be back at the bridges over the river. Below is the detail.	
	Stay on the main path. There will be many paths branching off to the left and right, the 'main' path is the wide path, stay on it, just continue ahead. You will go downhill, then slightly uphill for a long way, they steeply downhill.
26	At the bottom of the hill (the exact point at which you stop walking downhill and start going slightly uphill) the main path continues ahead, sometimes the tracks of large vehicles make it look as if the main path curves left, it doesn't – continue ahead.

32	Cross the lane (Rousebarn Lane) into woodland (Horrocks Wood).	
	Dtr	If you were to turn right into the lane and keep going to the end (6mns) then turn left, you will see a nice pub ahead, The Clarendon Arms (see the photo on page 67). From here, there is no need to retrace your steps back along the road. Instead: almost opposite the pub (slightly back the way you came) is a footpath signed *Croxley Green*. Continue to the end of the path, through two gates (past the *No Horse Riding…* sign), you are at "38" below, but from now on, please add 4 minutes to my times.
38	At the crossroads, turn left onto the track (if you are tall and can see the crossroads a few yards ahead, you may cut the corner off and save yourself 20 seconds).	
	39	Ahead through two gates (past the *No Horse Riding…* sign).
	44	Through the gate and continue ahead.
44	Turn left immediately after the barn, signed *Public footpath Rousebarn Lane ¾*.	
Summary of the remainder of the walk: at every choice, continue ahead until you get back to Cassiobury Park.		
	1:01	Ahead, alongside open field.
	1:06	Across the lane into woodland, signed *Public footpath 31 leading to Cassiobury Park 820 Yards*, steeply uphill.
	1:09	Continue exactly ahead, across a golf course (this *is* a public footpath!).
	1:12	Ahead into woodland.
	1:14	Ahead at crossroads, crossing a single-track road.
	✤	There are many single-track roads criss-crossing the golf course, most of them don't go anywhere in particular. This one goes nowhere in particular to your left, but to the right it goes all the way to Croxley.
	1:16	Ahead across a golf course (again) and into woodland, very steeply downhill.
1:18	Cross the bridge over the canal, then the bridge over the river	
1:20	then you are back at the picnic benches where you started	

WHIPPENDELL WOOD, CHANDLERS CROSS
AND THE LONG WAY BACK, PERIMETER PATH OF WHIPPENDELL WOOD
About 2 hours

mns	DIRECTIONS (for key see page 99)
	Start at the picnic benches by the river and canal (see page 23), cross the bridge over the river then cross the bridge over the canal, continue ahead for 20 paces
2	and turn right signposted *PUBLIC FOOTPATH 30*
13	There's a picnic bench on your left and a choice of three paths into Whippendell wood. Take the path ahead, passing to the right of the map.
	Stay on the main path. There will be many paths branching off to the left and right, the 'main' path is the wide path, stay on it, continue ahead at every choice.
32	Cross the lane (Rousebarn Lane) into woodland (Horrocks Wood)
	After 10 paces turn right.
37	At the end turn left.
	Dtr	Instead of turning left, turn right. The path ends at a road junction, turn left, The Clarendon Arms is at the crossroads, see picture.

41	Ahead through two gates (past the *No Horse Riding...* sign)
46	Through the gate and continue ahead.
	❖	The playground belongs to Redheath School, the farm is Oak Farm.
	Turn left immediately after the barn, signed *Public footpath Rousebarn Lane ¾*.
	↩	A shortcut back: if, instead of turning right, continue ahead, and take care to continue exactly ahead at every choice (including crossing the golf course twice) you will be back in 35 minutes.

	There is woodland across the field to your left, then woodland ahead.
59	When you get to the woodland ahead, turn left through the gate, arrow on gate reads, *Whippendell Woods Circular Walk 4*.
1:01	Fork right.
1:03	Through the little car park and ahead across the lane…
	✴ You are on Rousebarn Lane at the junction of Merlin's Wood and Newland's Spring.
	…and past the post with the map.
1:05	At the crossroads turn left onto the main path.
1:07	Ahead at crossroads past the horsehead sign *uphill*.

1:17	At crossroads, ahead, uphill.	
	i	Does the gate to your left look familiar? This is the way you came.
	↺	A shortcut back (30mns) is to turn right (i.e. so that the gate is behind you). Memorise these three rules, then it's safe to put this book away: 1) if the path forks, take the right fork 2) whenever you come to a crossroads, continue ahead 3) when you get to the bin and picnic bench at the top of the hill, keep ahead on the main path (then across the golf course, you'll recognise it)
	The main path curves to the right (arrow on post for *Whippendell Wood Circular Walk 1*), with a deep pit to the right – **DO NOT GO THIS WAY!** Instead, keep left, keep the perimeter fence to your left.	
1:31	The path peters out, don't worry about it, just keep walking ahead and you will see a car park through the trees ahead.	
1:33	Turn right alongside the car park.	
	At the top of the hill at the end of the car park, turn right onto the track signed *Horse riders must keep to the perimeter track*.	
	then after 10 or 20 paces turn left off the track and into the woodland.	
	i	For the next 2 or 3 minutes the path is not clear, but you can't get lost – really! You are in a very narrow strip of woodland, with a lane (and, later, farmers' fields) to your left, and the neat lawns of a golf course to your right. So providing you don't cross the lane or wander onto the golf course (or turn back the way you came) you can't get lost, keep ahead and after 2 or 3mns you will be on the path.
	The path will skirt the golf course, then there's a pit to your right	
1:46	then keep left. You should see open fields through the trees to your left.	
	Continue downhill	
1:49	and turn right onto the canal path	
1:58	to the lock.	
	Cross the bridge across the canal and continue ahead, across the bridge over the river	
2:00	to the picnic benches where you started.	

WETLAND WALK AND BACK ALONG THE CANAL
About 25 minutes

The circular route involves crossing the canal by walking over lock gates (they are narrow, you have to hold onto the rail), or you can make it a non-circular walk by going back the way you came.

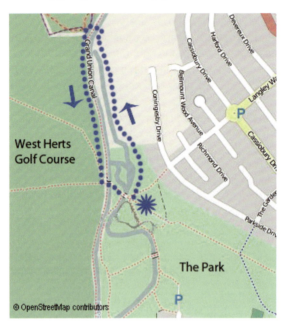

mns		DIRECTIONS (for key see page 9)
	\multicolumn{2}{l	}{Start at the picnic benches by the river and canal (see page 23), walk alongside the river (walk along the grass, not the path) keeping the river to your left, to the sign *Cassiobury Park Local Nature Reserve*.}
	Dtr	Thirty paces past the sign, fork right, continue for about 100 paces. This is the most secluded part of the park, known only to the park grounds men, a handful of locals, and children. What you will see are a series of ponds. To the un-initiated it's just mud and water, but look hard and you

		can see that everywhere is teaming with wildlife. Now retrace your steps.
	ff	The ponds are not natural. They are dug by local volunteers. They don't then 'fill them with water', they do nothing, water simply flows into them. Over time, trees grow around the edges, the ponds silt up and are no more, then volunteers dig more ponds. As you retrace your steps, look to your left, just after the war this area was allotments.
1½	and take the path ahead (the river is still to your left, but now hidden by woodland)	
3½	Turn left at the bench (across a small wooden walkway) then right, over a long wooden walkway.	
	Dtr	Alternatively, turn left at the bench as above, but then immediately left again, over another small wooden walkway, you are now on the island (see above "B" on the map on page 23, see "Explore the island" on the next page).
	i	You are now walking through a 'wetland nature reserve', with wooden walkways to take you across the wet bits. At times of drought you will see mostly parched earth, a little mud, and wonder what the walkways are for. If the season has been wet you will find yourself walking with water all around you (it really is spectacular). If the season has been wet *and* it has been raining heavily for days, this route will be flooded, you will have to turn back.
	ff	The streams around you (fast-moving mini rivers if the season is wet, mere trickles at times of drought) are chalk streams, fed from aquifers and bubble up through the chalk of the Chiltern Hills just a few miles to the North (though here the ground is 'London clay').
	Eventually the canal will be visible on your left	
	The path ends abruptly at a playing field and another sign (behind you as you leave the woodland) *Cassiobury Park Local Nature Reserve*.	
13	Turn left.	
14	At the trees turn left to the lock. Now either retrace your steps	
	or cross the canal by walking over the canal gate.	
14¼	On the other side of the canal turn left so that you are walking with the canal to your left.	
24	Cross the canal at the brick bridge by the lock.	
25	Cross the river.	
25½	Back at the picnic benches.	

EXPLORE THE ISLAND (optional)

A few yards after crossing the extra small wooden walkway, the footpath disappears. In the summer you will have to battle your way through thick undergrowth and climb over fallen trees; in the early spring or late autumn you will sink ankle-deep in mud; at times of flooding it will be impassable. If, however, you persevere, you will find your way to the middle of the island where there are two weirs with the remains of walls and ironwork. This was once a water mill.

Walk alongside the river by the weir, if it isn't too wet you'll be able to get off the island without having to retrace your steps. If you do get off the island you will re-join the path, then re-join my walk where you turn left at '13'; if you don't get off the island you will have live on fish and nettles until rescued by a passing barge.

The fact that, on the island, there are no paths this year does not mean that there will be no paths next year – paths (and streams) change over the years.

WOODLAND PARALLEL WITH CANAL (JUST NORTH OF THE PARK)
Then uphill to Whippendell Wood, about 45mns

mns	**DIRECTIONS** (for key see page 9)
0	Start at the picnic benches by the river and canal (see page 23), take the bridge over the river then the bridge over the canal and continue ahead for 10 paces.
2	then turn right signposted *PUBLIC FOOTPATH 30*.
7	You are going to turn right onto a narrow path into the woodland. But make sure it's the right path: it is just 50 paces before it crosses a single-track road, if you're tall you will see it ahead, if you're not sure, keep going until you see it (or walk up to it, turn back, count 50 paces, turn left into the woodland).
	When you find yourself going uphill you will (if you have a sense of direction) be aware that you are walking away from the canal.
	You can't get lost (honestly!), you are walking along a narrow strip of woodland, with a lane to your right and the golf course to your left. But whenever there's a choice of paths, keep left rather than right. You will

	walk in and out of the woodland on the edge of the golf course, you will hear the occasional sound of cars on the lane (which you can see in the winter when the trees are bare), you should be going uphill.
24	At the top the ground levels (you are definitely not going uphill any more), there's a slight clearing, for most of the year the path is not clear. Continue ahead for a few yards, you will come to a track.
27	Turn left onto the track it's a bridleway, look out for horses.
i	Not sure if you've come out of the woodland in the right place? When you get to the track, look to the right, you should see the barrier to the car park. If you can't see it, it's because you've come out of the woodland a few yards to the right, walk round the car park until you see the barrier, stand with your back to the barrier…and walk forward!

33	Follow the track left past a picnic bench and a sign to Cassiobury Park.
	Careful as you cross the golf course.

ff	You are *supposed* to stop, look right, and if you see golfers about to hit (drive) the ball, wait. And they are supposed to look, see you crossing, and wait. It doesn't always work. And they once shouted at me for walking too slowly.

45	Bridge to your left. cross the canal (or walk down to the lock to watch the boats)
	and over the bridge over the river
	to the picnic benches.

WOODLAND PARALLEL WITH CANAL (JUST NORTH OF THE PARK)

About 25mns Then either back along canal or along wetland nature reserve

mns	DIRECTIONS (for key see page 9)
	Start at the picnic benches by the river and canal (see page 23), cross both bridges and continue ahead for 10 paces
2	then turn right signposted *PUBLIC FOOTPATH 30*
6½	You are going to turn right onto a narrow path into the woodland. But make sure it's the right path: it is just 50 paces before it crosses a single-track road, if you're tall you will see it ahead, if you're not sure, keep going until you see it (or walk up to it, turn back, count 50 paces, turn left into the woodland).
8	Keep in a straight line across the clearing (at some times of year the path is clear, at other times it's not) - the path continues on the other side of the clearing, downhill.
13	You can see, ahead through the trees, open fields, as the path turns left and uphill, but you must turn *right* – downhill, you will see the fields to your left, you are looking across Charlotte's Vale (see the picture on the next page).

1.0 P.m.   2. -3.30 FRIDAY

RUTH.   Linon £25.

P. ~~76~~.

~~P. 76~~

P. 53

P. 42

Benefit - Wisconsin.

No we cannot the
others once is overshadowed
A Development under.
epidemic more than usually
funds inflicting the
environment.

The Idol must be kept as
a community meeting
place. It has been there
after people are aware of
so great for their mental
health. Private lessons Piano
2 or 7 Pink Try Denton.
11/31 "   2:40
1 82
850727 Gift Card $50 ?   8270058 ?
Verification code:

August 1 MCMLXXII

	ℹ	You are going the wrong way if you are heading uphill and see, on your left (in quick succession): deep pit with a grass embankment on the other side, then the open grass of a golf course…and you are still going uphill. Turn round and follow the path downhill, stay on the path with the open fields to your left, always downhill.
16		Arrive at the canal

There are now two ways back, along the canal path all the way:

	16	**Turn RIGHT onto the canal path.**
	25	Turn left over the bridge over the canal.
		then continue ahead over the bridge over the river
	26½	and you are back at the picnic benches where you started.

Or cross the canal and walk back through the wetland nature reserve.

	16	**Turn LEFT onto the canal path**
		and at the lock cross the canal by walking *carefully* over the lock gate
		then ahead for a few paces then turn right, continue ahead towards the fields
	17	and turn right by the sign *Cassiobury Park Local Nature Reserve*
	ℹ	At times of floods, the path becomes a lake. You could turn round, go back, and follow the canal path instead. Alternatively: move a few yards to your left and continue (parallel to the path) by the stream, you will arrive at a zig-zag walkway (pretty, with water flowing on all sides).
		After the long wooden walkway is a short wooden walkway, then the path ends at a bench,
	26	turn right, you can see the picnic benches in the distance ahead

TWO WALKS ALONG THE CANAL AND ALONG *THE GROVE*

At *The Grove*, the smaller dots and arrows are for the shorter (1 hour) walk and the larger dots and arrows are for the longer (1½ hour) walk.

You must, of course, walk along the canal path both ways.

CANAL NORTH, THEN THROUGH *THE GROVE,* about 1 hour

mns		DIRECTIONS
		Start at the picnic benches by the river and canal (see page 23), cross the river, cross the canal, turn right onto the canal path. You should be walking with the canal to your right.
16		Cross the canal (wooden-railed bridge).
21		Under *Bridge 165* (by the white cottage).
26		Under *Bridge 164* (White bridge marked *The Grove Bridge*).
		Cross the canal, *Bridge 163*.
30		and immediately on the other side, turn sharp left onto the public footpath (yellow arrow on post) so that you double back. Keep left, keep close to the canal.
31		Cross the path and continue ahead (beware of golfers) to the post with the yellow footpath arrow, and keep going, towards the buildings below the woodland.
33		As you get to the beautifully-manicured grass of the golf course, turn sharp right ("Sarratt" arrow on post).
36		Ahead at the crossroads, the path becomes a track.
38		As the track curves left, turn *right* (white arrow on post).
40		At the post, you have a choice of routes back to the canal (same distance to within 30 seconds). Fork left if you prefer the canal path, fork right if you prefer the semi-woodland by the golf course.
either	40	Fork left.
	40½	Turn right onto the canal path.
	43½	Lock.
	46½	The white 'hump back' bridge where you originally left the canal.
or	40	Fork right.
	42	Fork left (arrow on post) towards the white-ish structure.
	46	That white-ish thing turns out to be the bridge where you originally left the canal, turn right onto the canal path.
1:06		at the lock by the brick bridge, at Cassiobury Park, cross the bridge
1:08		and continue ahead to cross the bridge over the river to the picnic benches.

CANAL NORTH, THROUGH *THE GROVE*, about 1½ hours

mns	DIRECTIONS (for key see page 9)
	Start at the picnic benches by the river and canal (see page 23), cross the river, cross the canal, turn right onto the canal path. You should be walking with the canal to your right.
16	Cross the canal (wooden-railed bridge).
21	Under *Bridge 165* (by the white cottage).
26	Under *Bridge 164* (White bridge marked *The Grove Bridge*).
	Cross the canal, *Bridge 163*, hump-back bridge (joggers and cyclist struggle over this one!)
30	and immediately on the other side, turn sharp left between the posts (yellow arrow) onto the footpath, so that you double back. Keep left, keep close to the canal
31	Cross the tarmac path onto the grass (beware of golfers) and continue ahead to the post with the yellow footpath arrow, and keep going, towards the buildings below the woodland.

33	As you get to the beautifully-manicured grass of the golf course, turn sharp right (arrow on post, but no longer yellow).
36	Ahead at the crossroads, the path becomes an earth track, follow it left, round the garden then uphill.
40	At the crossroads continue ahead / slightly right, up the hill (there are two paths, they run parallel, but take the left path). Notice the concrete strips either side of the path, ignore them, continue ahead.
42	then after the second set of concrete strips count 50 paces and turn left into the woods (by a tall tree, at a gap in the holly).
	ff You could have turned left earlier but I've taken you further up the hill so that you can look back and admire the view. The big road is a motorway link road linking the M25 (at Junction 19) with the A41. I'm not sure if the industrial buildings, beyond, are on the outskirts of Abbots Langley or if they are behind Leavesden Studios (where you can have tours of the Harry Potter studios).
46	At the end turn left.
	Keep right to the playing field and across the yard. Ahead to your left is a greenhouse and a long wall, walk alongside the wall. Look through the gate and admire the walled garden
49½	Turn left at the corner, keep following the wall.
51	At the very end of the path turn right onto the car-park-road.
52	then left between the two wooden posts into the woodland
	At the end turn right onto the road
53	then left towards open land
56½	and onto the road, downhill, through the golf course (stay on the road, do not stray, this is a private golf course!).
1:00	Cross the road bridge carefully, the left side parapet is safest.
	On the other side of the bridge, cross the road and take the steep path from the bridge down to the canal.
1:03	You should be walking along the canal path with the canal to your right
	At the lock by the brick bridge cross over the canal.
	and continue ahead and cross the bridge over the river
1:30	to the picnic benches

THE CANAL PATH

The attraction of a canal walk is that you can't get lost. And you can turn round whenever you want. And it's *relatively* flat. Actually, you walk uphill if you are heading North (towards the Chiltern Hills) and downhill if you are heading South (towards London).

CANAL SOUTH

mns	**DIRECTIONS** (for key see page 9)
0	Start at the picnic benches by the river and canal (see page 23).
	Cross the bridge over the river, then keep ahead over the bridge over the canal, and as you leave the bridge turn left down the slope.
2	You should be walking with the canal to your left.
14	Bridge 68 is the last bridge across the canal back into the park, you are now leaving Cassiobury Park.

		Take a closer look at the lake on the other side. Cross the bridge (Bridge 68), continue for 50 yards, look through the fence. It's Croxley Green Watercress Farm, the 'lakes' separated by concrete divisions are watercress silt pits. Now return to the canal.
	Dtr	
16	Cassio Bridge Lock (Lock No.78)	
18	Railway bridge.	
	✲	Metropolitan Line from Croxley to Watford.

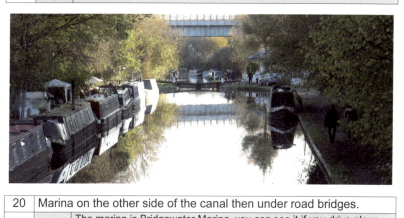

20	Marina on the other side of the canal then under road bridges.	
	✲	The marina is Bridgewater Marina, you can see it if you drive along the A412 / Watford Road between the roundabout at Ascot Road (where the industrial estates are) and the roundabout at Baldwins Lane (the lane to Sarrat and Loudwater) – you may have noticed boats and wondered where they were located.
	ff	See the exotic garden (on other side) marked CASSIO WHARF.
22	Under railway bridge. 2013: disused. But will carry the new *Croxley Link* railway, due to open 2016.	
In the next few minutes there are several sights of minor interest.		
	ff	Notice the sign, "Grand Union Canal Walk", London one way (about 10 miles), Birmingham the other way (about 90 miles). To walk this route, stay on the canal path, no signposts needed.
	ff	The large building on the left with the pitched roof (just visible through the trees in the Summer, more obvious in the Winter) is a joinery business by Croxley Business Park. Several thousand people

		work on the Croxley and Watford Business Parks, most of them probably have no idea that there is open countryside nearby.
	⊕	The housing estate on the other side of the canal - where is it? If you have reason to go to the Business Parks at Croxley, you will find that the entrance to the estates is at the roundabout at the end of Ascot Road, the first exit is Watford Business Park, the second exit goes to Croxley Business Park, the third exit doesn't appear to go anywhere. It goes to the canal and to this estate, ending at Common Moor, Croxley, which you will see shortly.
34	↺	Emergency Escape Route. Immediately before the lock, take the path signed *Croxley Station*. Walk uphill for 2mns to the main road (and look back at the view!) then you will see the station ahead (another 1½mns), it's on the other side of the road, cross carefully. Your journey from the canal to the picnic benches will probably be 5 or 10 minutes quicker than walking, it depends on how long you have to wait for a train.
35	Common Moor Lock (the moor is Common Moor).	

	Dtr	Take the path (by the lock) up into the woods, there's a clearing with benches overlooking the canal and common, a nice place for a picnic.
	ff	Can you see cows on the common? This is 'common' land, which

		means it doesn't belong to anyone, which means (by ancient rights) anyone can graze cattle on it. And they do! Though it tends to be local farmers because the inhabitants of Croxley don't keep cows in their gardens.
48	Under railway bridge by pylons.	
	✳	Metropolitan Line between Rickmansworth and Moor Park.
	✳	Don't be fooled by the footpath sign, *High Street ¾*. It's over a mile to Rickmansworth High Street. Croxley *is* closer, but it doesn't have a High Street.
51	Lock No.80. Lot Mead.	
	✳ **i**	*Croxley Green Boundary Walk* (by the Croxley Residents Association) takes you on a 6.3 mile walk around Croxley, see http://www.croxleyresidentsassociation.co.uk/boundary-walk.html - nice map but the route isn't marked and there are no directions, so you'll have to hope that all the signs are intact and pointing the right way.
52	Under low bridge.	
	Path becomes a bridge over a little weir.	
	↺	The lakes to the right are flooded quarries, some are now used as watercress farms, the next two paths to the right will take you round the lakes and along the River Colne.
	ff	Look at the boats on the other side of the canal, notice the sheds and little gardens, these are permanent homes at Batchworth Long Term Moorings.
1:06	Lock No.81. Batchworth Lock.	
	The bridge at the lock crosses a small canal 'arm'. When you come back, remember to take the right hand fork across this same bridge, because the 'arm' is just a dead end.	
	i	Refreshments and picnic tables to your right, a pub on the other side (cross the bridge).
1:07	Under road bridge 174.	
	i	The sign to Ebury Way: this is where the Ebury Way ends (or starts, if you're starting from here). The other end is at Oxhey Park near Bushey Station, six miles away.
	✳	This road (on the bridge) is in the middle of Rickmansworth, it is the A404 / London Road at the Batchworth Roudabout, to the West it goes to Chorleywood and the M25 at Junction 18, to East it

		branches, either Tolpits Lane (local road to Watford), or the A404 (up the steep hill) to Northwood, Pinner, Hatch End and Stanmore.
	ff	On the wall under the bridge is painted a silhouette of a horse pulling a barge. This is how heavy goods were moved in the 18th and 19th centuries. Barges didn't have engines, they were towed by horses, which is why a canal path is called a towpath. But most people don't know this, so in this book I call it a 'canal path' rather than a 'towpath'.
	Dtr	The path to the right goes into the middle of Rickmansworth Aquadrome (for the car park and toilets), it is mostly water, but is quite large (the size of Cassiobury Park plus a little bit of Whippendell Wood). So feel free to make a detour, enjoy a picnic, swimming, boating etc, but I leave it to you to find your way back to the canal.
1:13	Under road bridge 174	
	✦	On this side of the canal the road goes to the car park in the Aquadrome, on the other side it goes to a side street and then the front entrance of Tesco.
	ff	The strip of land alongside the canal (just the first six feet feet) belong not to the houses and shops, but to the Canal & River Trust, and so when they built Tesco the arrangement was for those few feet to be used for mooring for Tesco customers.
	✦	The car park through the trees to the right is the car park in Rickmansworth Aquadrome.
1:22	Lock No.82. Stockers Lock.	
	The footpath goes to the southern tip of Rickmansworth Aquadrome.	
	✦	Where does the canal go from here? It eventually runs into the Thames at Brentford. But if you were to take the Paddington Arm the route is: Southall, Alperton, Kensal Green and Ladbrook Grove; at Little Venice it goes through the Maida Vale Tunnel into Regents Park (becoming the Regents Park Canal); then the three locks at Camden (exit here for Camden Market); Kings Cross (Battle Bridge Basin); the Islington Tunnel, the City of London and into the River Thames at Limehouse. A popular route is then up the Thames to Brentford and back North…and back to Rickmansworth.
	ff	At Park Royal the canal goes over the North Circular Road, the viaduct looks like just another bridge from the road, drivers have no idea that boats are floating over their heads.

CANAL NORTH

mns	DIRECTIONS (for key see page 9)	
	Start at the picnic benches by the river and canal (see page 23).	
	Cross the bridge over the river, then keep ahead over the bridge over the canal, and as you leave the bridge turn sharp right down to the canal path.	
2	You are at the lock by the park.	
	ff	This is Lock No.77, *Iron Bridge Lock*. There is a bridge 10 yards from the lock, it is called *The Rustic Bridge*, it is not particularly 'rustic' and is certainly is not made of iron. And if you need to describe it to boaters, you must say, "The bridge where the children wave".
8	**i**	The bench on the left is a 10 minute walk for those who walk *really* slowly, a nice stroll for those who can't walk far, get them to sit on this bench for a rest before going back to the park.

You are approaching the next lock, see picture below.	
11	The path becomes a bridge, with water to your left (looks like a big pond if the season is dry, like a river after heavy rain).

12	Lock No. 76, Cassiobury Park Lock.	
	ff	Note the white lock keepers cottage, sign reads, *Danger Crocodiles*. The fields opposite are playing fields, used by (amongst others) Watford Grammar School for Boys, and Fullerians Rugby Club. Incidentally, there are no crocodiles. But it may be wise not to tell this to small children. The threat of crocodiles might keep them from getting too close to the edge. (Just an idea).
	ff	On your left (on the canal path) a post reads, *C J C Co. Braunston 71 Miles*. Here's an activity to keep small children amused: during the walk you will see a few mileposts like these, all giving the distance to Braunston. How many?
	ff	Braunston is near Rugby and Daventry, on the way to Birmingham. Its significance is that it's the junction of the Grand Union Canal and the Oxford Canals, the 1830s equivalent of the M1 / M6 motorway junction.

14	Lock No.75, Cassiobury Park Top Lock.	
	ff	It is even further from the park than the previous lock. It's not that the park has moved, rather that this was once *all* Cassiobury.
15	Long concrete channel (about 40m long) taking the overflow from the canal.	
	ff	Canals do not flood, they have systems (usually weirs) to remove excess water. Sometimes, here, the water is just a trickle. My photo was taken after heavy rain and melting snow.

16	Cross the wooden-railed bridge, Bridge 166, Rough Wood Bridge.
21	Under *Bridge 165* (by the white cottage), Grove Mill Bridge.
	The bridge carries a road, *Grove Mill Lane*. To the right it goes to the A411 Hempstead Road; to the left it goes past Whipendell Wood, then at the end you can turn left to Chandlers Cross or right to Langlebury and Hunton Bridge.
26	Under *Bridge 164*, a white bridge marked *The Grove Bridge*. Though it's called *Grove Ornamental Bridge*, so as not to be confused with the previous bridge.

		The bridge carries a narrow lane, to the right it winds its way back to the A411 Hempstead Road, to the left it cuts through the golf course at The Grove (*Luxury 5-Star Hotel, Spa and Golf Course*). If you want to take just a little peak, walk up the slope, cross the bridge (carefully!) then continue for 50 paces, you will see the golf course, the lakes and the house. When you walk back to the canal, stand on the bridge and admire the view.

30	Cross the canal, *Bridge 163*, Lady Capel's Bridge (joggers and cyclist struggle over this one!).	
	i	At this bridge, it *looks* as if the path continues ahead and not over the bridge, but that will merely take you to the gardens of those nice houses (see the picture at the top of the next page).

	i	A few gardens further along, notice how the canal is wider, this is *Lady Capel's Winding Hole.* The horses that pulled the barges were confined to the towpath (on one side of the canal) and so couldn't turn a barge round to face the other way. So the sailors had to erect a sale and rely on the wind, hence "winding hole".
33		Lock No.74, Lady Capel lock (the noise of traffic, from now on, is from the A41).
	ff	*Elizabeth Capel (nee Morrison) was the heir of Sir Charles Morrison of Cassiobury. She married Arthur Capel in 1627, inherited his grandfather's estates in 1632, and the couple became one of the wealthiest in England.* To see portrait of Elizabeth, scan QR code No.8 on page 98.
37		Under road bridge. This is "Junction 19 Road Bridge" named after an unmemorable junction of the M25.

		It's not actually *at* Junction 19 of the M25, it's at the huge roundabout at the top of the A411 Hempstead Road, where ahead is the A41 towards Kings Langley and Hemel Hempstead, to the right is the A41 into London, and to the left (which is where you are standing) is the *slip-road* onto the M25 at Junction 19.
	ff	The canal path curves away from the canal past masses of reeds, this *might* be a dried-up winding hole…but I'm not sure. Look at the massive rusted bolts, I think there must have been something interesting here. At the very corner, there's a footpath off to the left (don't' take it!) which is of no significance except that I took the nice photograph, below.

44	Under road bridge, *Watford Road Bridge* (A41).
46	Lock No.73, Hunton Bridge Bottom Lock.
	Private footbridge, goes to the lock keepers cottage.
48	Lock No72, Hunton Bridge Top Lock.

53	Under road bridge, Hunton Bridge No.162
	i Sign on bridge reads, *Dog & Partridge 100 yards then turn left*. Climb the embankment, turn right onto the pavement, *The Kings Head* pub and *The Coach House Coffee Shop* are on the right (2mns), or continue to the mini roundabout and turn right (another minute) for Harry's. I couldn't find The Dog and Partridge.
	ff When you walk back to the bridge, look ahead over the junction at St Paul's Church, built in 1864 by a local, William Lloyd, a student of William Butterfield who built Keble College, Oxford, named after the Victorian clergyman John Keble, who was no relation to the Kebbell family who built Carpenders Park on the Southern outskirts of Watford, which was the subject of the novel *Tropic of Ruislip* by Leslie Thomas, about wife-swapping in 1970s suburbia.
52	Lock No.71, Home Park Farm Lock.
1:08	Under bridge 160, the Kings Langley Motorway Bridge (M25 J20), at the junction of the A41, Kings Langley immediately to the North, Abbots Langley immediately to the East. Notice how bit the bridge is, there's even a farm and a river underneath it.

	ff	Notice the wind turbine to your right, it's located at the UK headquarters of a company that makes wind turbines.
1:14	Under Bridge 159 immediately followed by road Bridge 158A immediately followed by Lock No.70, Home Park Mill Lock	
	✴	The road is Home Park Mill Link Road, which links the High Street in Kings Langley with nothing in particular (a couple of small industrial estates) – very close to Kings Langley Station. You are now in the heart of industrial Kings Langley.
	ff	The big lake is a trout fishery. Peering up from the trees is a model of a dinosaur (not the best way to scare away poachers).
1:25	Road bridge 158, Water Lane Bridge. The canal path runs out. Walk up onto the bridge, turn right onto the road (no need to cross the road!) and down the other side, so that you are on the other side of the canal.	
1:27	Lock No.69A, Kings Langley Lock.	
1:29	Bridge 157, made of blue iron. This bridge really doesn't have a name, it's at Kings Langley, shall we call it the Blue Bridge, and hope they don't repaint it?	
	ff	The 'river' to your left is not a river, it's part of the canal, the *Home Park Arm*. Many new developments (2013) on the other side of the canal, both commercial and residential.

1:43	Conveyor contraption followed by rail Bridge No.156, Kings Langley Skew Railway Bridge.
1:45	Factory Pipe bridge.
1:48	Bridge No 155, Red Lion Lane Bridge, you need to cross the canal, either by crossing the road bridge…
1.48½	…or by continuing to the Lock 69, Nash Mill Bottom Lock, and carefully crossing the lock gate.
	Under footbridge to new development
1:51	to Lock 68, Nash Mill Top Lock
	i The Red Lion pub nearby has an entrance on the canal path. This is also the site of a large boot sale.

THE WALK BACK

If you've got this far, congratulations, you are now half way through the walk. Now all you have to do is to turn round and walk back. At any point, you can see how far you have to go by referring back through the last few pages and reading the times (bridge numbers are the easiest landmarks). Here are some of the landmarks:

Bridge 160, about an hour to go.

Bridge 163, about 30mns to go.

Bridge 165, about 20mns to go.

QR CODES AND URLs

If you are out walking, scan these QR codes with your mobile device; if you are at home in front of a computer, type in the URL; if you are not very good at computers and don't know what these are, then please ignore this section.

THIS BOOK
www.cassiobury-walks.co.uk

See a new selection of photographs each season, plus extra walks and information.
You can even leave feedback!

1

2

CASSIOBURY PARK
www.cassioburypark.info/

Everything you need to know about the park including special events, nature trails, activities for children.

FRIENDS OF CASSIOBURY PARK
www.friendsofcassioburypark.org.uk/

FoCP liaise with the council to represent the interests of park users. Volunteer working parties pick up litter and work with *Herts&Middlesex Widlife Trust* to clear silted-up streams, dig ponds and help plant trees and hedges.

3

4

CASSIOBURY PARK RESTORATION PROJECT
www.watford.gov.uk/ccm/content/leisure-and-community/cassiobury-park-heritage-lottery-fund-restoration.en

See the latest information about the restoration of Cassiobury Park & Whippendell Wood

5	**HERTS & MIDDX WILDLIFE TRUST** http://www.hertswildlifetrust.org.uk/NatureReserves/Local/cassiobury Find out about the wildlife	

	THE MINIATURE RAILWAY www.miniaturerailwayworld.co.uk/Watford.html Latest opening times, history of each locomotive	9

6	**THE WEATHER** *www.bbc.co.uk/weather* This QR takes you to the forecast for London, which I find more accurate for this area than the forecast for Watford.	

	**TRAFFIC INFORMATION** www.trafficengland.com/index.aspx Worried about getting home? The *Highways Agency* website. Traffic alerts; the average speed of traffic on every section of every motorway; live feeds of motorway cameras.	7

8	**LADY CAPEL** www.gogmsite.net/_Media/ca_1655_elizabeth_capell_co.jpg The Capel family were based in Cassiobury in the 1630s (see page 91), here is a portrait of Lady Capel.